CONQUERING THE MOUNTAIN CALLED ME

By Sharon C. B. Hunter

BK Royston Publishing
P. O. Box 4321
Jeffersonville, IN 47131
502-802-5385
http://www.bkroystonpublishing.com
bkroystonpublishing@gmail.com

© Copyright – 2017

All Rights Reserved. No part of this book may be reproduced, stored in a retrieval system, or transmitted by any means without the written permission of the author.

Cover Design: Brent Barnett
Cover Image © Shutterstock.com by permission and standard license

ISBN: 978-1-946111-37-1

Printed in the United States of America

Dedication

I dedicate this book to my Father, John A. Cummins. You have been an awesome provider. You provided food when we needed it. You provided shelter all our lives. You provided wisdom and spiritual guidance throughout my life.

I remember when I was really going through an emotional time. You listened to me whine and moan. Although I cannot repeat all the words you used, I understood the context of what you said that day and I still live by it as an adult Christian woman.

I would also like to dedicate this book to every person that helped me grow as a Woman of God. Sitting under some of you was not always easy, but it was important to my maturity as God's Woman.

Thank you all and bless you abundantly!

Keep serving the Master and teaching others to develop, mature and serve Him as well

Graciously submitted, Pastor Sharon C B Hunter

Acknowledgements

I want to always acknowledge my husband; Pastor Dominic Hunter, who is the love and a blessing in my life. You always are so encouraging. Thank you.

I want to thank my children; Danielle, John G Lamont, Gwendolyn, Charmaine, Phillip and Jasmine for pushing me to my dreams, pulling me into my reality and encouraging me to do it all over again if I did not get my desired results. Thank You.

Lastly, I would like to thank my circle of family, friends and church family that continues to support and encourage me that dreams can become reality through Jesus Christ.

Table of Contents

DEDICATION	iii
ACKNOWLEDGEMENTS	v
INTRODUCTION	ix
FEED IT, FACE IT, AND FIX IT	1
OVERCOME SELF TO SERVE	13
FOLLOW GOD'S ORDERED STEPS	29
NO MAN OR WOMAN IS AN ISLAND	43
FOLLOW GPS-GOD'S POSITIONING SYSTEM	53
AVOIDING THE SLUDGE OF COULDA', SHOULDA', AND WOULDA'	65
GET OVER IT!	83
WHAT MAKES US MORE THAN CONQUERORS?	97
CONQUER FEARS	109
CONQUER THE FEAR OF FAILURE	117

CONQUER FEAR WHEN GOD'S OPPORTUNITY KNOCKS   125

CONQUERING THE MOUNTAIN CALLED ME   135

Introduction

What if you walked into a 1st grade classroom, and saw a 12th grader sitting in a tiny desk. Wouldn't that look strange? I believe it would cause a litany of questions as to why this student was not among his or her peers, and why they have not developed and moved forward.

As Christians, we may look like this 12th grader in the first grade when we refuse to learn how to move forward from self-sabotaging decisions, past mistakes and even problematic situations that cause us to live beneath abundant living.

Conquering the Mountain called ME is an in-depth look at how the Word of God through the Holy Spirit can teach us how to conquer our mountains of personal pitfalls that hold us back.

This book encourages the reader to move forward from bad choices, bad situations and even bad people. Conquering the Mountain called me also encourages Christians and potential Christians to ask the question, "What am I supposed to learn from this issue?" In other words, how can I develop, and what can I learn from this bad choice? Each time we seek insight and wisdom, the Holy Spirit takes time to teach us about our character defects, flaws and shortcomings as well as triumphs, strengths and anointing. He puts forth the effort to teach us, if we put forth the effort to want to learn how to put in the work and develop as Christians.

Conquering the Mountain called ME, is not a book that will answer all your questions. AS a matter of fact; once you conquer something inside of yourself and become better, there will always be other projects that need attention. However, the goal of this book is to encourage the reader to take a self-inventory and look at opportunities to develop as a Man or Woman of God. I encourage you to invest some time in pursuing the chapters of this book and learn how to 'Conquer the Mountain called ME.'

CONQUERING THE MOUNTAIN CALLED ME

CHAPTER 1
FEED IT, FACE IT, AND FIX IT

1 John4:3 "But every spirit who does not acknowledge Jesus is not from God. This is the spirit of the antichrist. You have heard that he is coming, and now he is already in the world."

1 John 4:4 "Little children, you belong to God and have overcome them, because the one who is in you is greater than the one who is in the world."

There is an old joke that asks the question, 'how do you eat an elephant?' Some people take the question at face value and apply the analytical approach. They attempt to break the information up into parts. They even go into detail about how to prepare the animal for consumption. Others try to put together an elaborate strategy that may make the problem more complex than it needs to be because it is a joke. However, there are some people that are able to see beyond the enormity of the animal, and they get it's a joke! So, they answer correctly, 'one bite at a time!' And although the joke may make you giggle, there is some truth hidden in the core thought that we should receive about life. Life must be lived one step at a time. Don't misunderstand; there will be things that provoke us to take everything fast and in a multi- task nature. However, the reality is that we should not be trying to fix everything all at once. We have to deal with the issues one at a time and one step at a time. The steps we take to overcome the issues may feel like an uphill mountain journey on an icy slope. So,

CONQUERING THE MOUNTAIN CALLED ME

without the correct tools, we can't climb and conquer the mountain.

Now, depending on who you are talking to they will tell you the tallest mountain from base to peak is Mount Mauna Kea on the island of Hawaii. However, over half of the mountain is submerged. Others may say Mount Everest is the tallest mountain above sea level. In either case, there is a mountain that you and I climb every day that is higher than both of these natural phenomena. It is the mountain called me! We should always be looking for ways to better ourselves and carve out for ourselves a better self. Climbing higher personal heights takes effort and discipline that will help us be better human beings but we have to want this change. The dreams and visions we see for our lives are available but we have to be willing to take a long look at ourselves and change if necessary. This change will help us move from existing to living, but we have to be willing to pursue God's plan for personal development. The heart of this book/conversation is to encourage those who want change and to introduce some insight that may help them start the climb called MOUNTAIN ME!

One of my spiritual fathers, Pastor D. Simpson, used to cry out loud and spared not from the pulpit "What you feed is what will lead." His passionate explanation assisted each person listening in taking an interest in what they fed their spirit.

1 John 4:3 reads, "But every spirit who does not acknowledge Jesus is not from God. This is the spirit of the antichrist. You have heard

that he is coming, and now he is already in the world."

Therefore, since the antichrist spirit is in the world it is available for all to feed and fill the spirit with deadly garbage. The garbage that people feed on can vary from heretic teachings, occult preaching, degrading music, pornographic material and the list continues. These things are saturated with spirits that do not acknowledge or uplift Jesus Christ and are not from God. Therefore when people feed on lies and deception strongholds build up like mountains. A stronghold is an incorrect thinking pattern that is contrary to the Word of God. People who consistently feed on this mess live their lives without a power source fueled by God's Word. And without the Word of God, it is impossible to tear down strongholds and maintain a healthy relationship with God. If God is not our power source, in the famous words of any astronaut to the NASA center, 'Houston there is a problem!'

When climbing a physical mountain a person runs the risk of falling rocks, falling ice, solar radiation and weather conditions that create problems. In the spiritual climb to personal improvement, lack of the correct power source will result in conditions that create unwanted repeat issues and downfalls that turn into ditches and pitfalls that become a grave. All because there is a failure to plug in and stay plugged into the correct power source.

So, then the spirit of the antichrist is the power source that leads and the proof of his leading can be seen on the news, in the newspaper, and even online. We are constantly bombarded with stories of children who were dumped in the garbage. There are women who were beaten to death and men who were violated by someone who did not possess the spirit of the Almighty God. This constant barrage of the enemy's tactics creates a stronghold and begins to desensitize people to the power of God. The spirit of the antichrist is here and there is a feeding frenzy of foolishness that leads to choices that kill, steal, and destroy. (John 10:10)

So, then the obvious question is, "How do you get people to feed on the right source that will tear down these strongholds?

1John 4:4 Little children, you belong to God and have overcome them, because the one who is in you is greater than the one who is in the world.

The main key to helping people feed on the right source is helping them to understand that they belong to God and that he helps those who belong to Him. I hear people say all the time, 'this is my truth.' Which this implies they have some sort of personal truth that is driving their life. However, when we accept Jesus as our personal Savior we embrace God's truth and absorb His ideas and knowledge. Therefore, as we digest God's Word and ingest all the nutrients of His Word, we feed on healthy spiritual food that becomes a catalyst for growth. The Word goes on to say that the one (God) who lives in us is Greater than the one who is in the world. So, then in the simplest terms, we have to choose to feed on the Word of God and allow the Word to lead us to a wealthy and healthy place or we can feed on the world that lacks nutrients and leads us to lowest form of self that does not represent value in family or community.

My current Pastor, Dominic Hunter, is also my husband. One of his favorite sayings is, 'We have to face it to fix it' and this is so true! If we are leading with the wrong values, morals, and attitudes, we have to face the fact that what we are doing is not working. It is not until we decide that we want more that we will strive for more. The "IT" we face will vary from person to person. Some people have relationship problems that they have to face. Others will have drug or drinking issues that they will have to address. The point is in an effort to fix our issues we have to face whatever IT is that blocks us from becoming better. It is equally important to understand that facing a problem with Christ Jesus at the forefront and fixing it does not mean that you will never face another problem. However, it does set us on the spiritual path that will help us remember what we learned and re-apply that learned information for the next "IT".

Climbing any mountain requires boots and crampons that dig into the mountain. So, then we have to put on our Gospel shoes and crampons that dig into the Word of God. The first step in CLIMBING THE MOUTAIN called ME is to make sure that we are feeding from the right source, Jesus Christ. It is so important that we realize the climb to our personal best is an ongoing climb that never ends and lastly, accepting the truth from the Word of God will help us FEED FROM THE RIGHT SOURCE, FACE OUR ISSUES AND TRUST GOD TO TEACH US HOW TO FIX IT!

CONQUERING THE MOUNTAIN CALLED ME

Are you feeding from the right source?
Are you facing problematic life issues that are holding you back?
Are you ready for God to help you fix it?
What are you doing to fix it?

NOTES

CHAPTER 2
OVERCOME SELF TO SERVE

Jeremiah 18:4 "But the vessel he was working on with the clay was ruined in the potter's hand. So, he remade it into another vessel that seemed appropriate to him."

I remember as a child growing up, there was a song that the children's choir sang at my grandmothers church. The lyrics of the song said, 'please be patient with me, God is not through with me yet...'' I can still hear the adolescent voices singing close to the correct key as they swayed back and forth. The people in the church would stand up and clap their hands to encourage the children. However, the words of the song were not just for the children, it was for anyone who was having a face-off with themselves in an effort to serve God.

As we strive to gain an understanding of feeding our spirit and fixing our issues, one of the most important revelations we will encounter is overcoming the self to serve God. As we stand before this first climb for our personal best on Mountain Me, there are three major things that we must explore.

1) We have to stop being against ourselves,
2) Avoid false fellowship and
3) Accept the personal stretch in an effort to overcome self in order to serve God.

Psalm 139:14 says, "... I will praise thee; for I am fearfully *and* wonderfully made: marvelous *are* thy works; and *that* my soul knoweth right well." David makes several self-affirmations in this text that declare his confidence in who God created him to be.

CONQUERING THE MOUNTAIN CALLED ME

He says"...for I am fearfully and wonderfully made..." David declares that in spite of whatever he looked like, God created him and he is beautiful. We must reverence God and His creation. When we look at any part of our bodies and begin to declare negative affirmations like, I hate my breasts, my teeth are ugly, my hair is too nappy or too straight, etc. etc. etc. we are making negative affirmations about ourselves and God's work. We are His masterpiece and how do we tell the master His masterpiece is a failure? We must love ourselves and embrace God's creation in us with great admiration and reverence. Also, we must walk in the knowledge that we are wonderfully made. It was God that decided your blue eyes and fair skin would be His design for you. However, that design is equally as beautiful as the brown eyed, dark skinned beauty that He also created. Everything God created us to be is beautiful and we can't discredit the work of the master who orchestrates our lives. God wants us to praise Him for the great work and effort He put into making us beautiful and whole. David also made the affirmation that he knew God's work was marvelous, and he knew it well. God wants each of us to know in our heart, mind, and soul that he created us to be marvelous. Therefore, we must cease and desist saying mean things about ourselves even if we say that we are saying it in fun. It is never fun to make fun of others including yourself! Another aspect of self-sabotage is indulging in activities that we know are not good for us or our health. The complexities of wrong choices go deep. They have an effect on our life's journey. The effects of self-sabotaging choices make a difference in the lives our life touches. Therefore, if you have continued bad habits it will eventually influence you and someone you love. We can become overwhelmed with drugs, drinking, self-sabotage and other problematic habits, and this creates a change that sucks up valuable time all because we did not value ourselves enough to stop being against ourselves.

Now that we have insight on self- sabotaging choices, let's look at avoiding false fellowship. 1 John 1:6-7 says "...If we say that we have fellowship with Him, and walk in darkness, we lie and do not practice the truth. But if we walk in the light as He is in the light, we have fellowship with one another, and the blood of Jesus Christ His son cleanses us from all sin...." We live in a time where people like to say that they are Christian. I believe this occurs because the main message of Christianity is love. So then people can be more trusting when you say that you are a Christian. However, the Bible clearly says, "try the spirit by the spirit' which means don't just believe a person because they say they have fellowship with God, watch their actions! When a person says they have a relationship with God, people look at them differently. We are told multiple places in the New Testament watch and pray, try the spirit by the spirit, and other Words of Truth that help us pay attention to the actions of others. People who say they have fellowship with God yet they are walking in darkness the Word of God calls them liars. The Word goes on to say such individuals do not practice the truth. All this means is they are not practicing the truth according to the Word of God. They have their personal justifications of why they live a life contrary to the Word of God and therefore live a life of darkness. The life we live represents the walk we have. So then if you are lying, backbiting, sowing discord, and the list goes on, this is a representation of walking in the dark. There are facets of darkness just like there are facets of light. People who wallow in rebellion, disobedience, bad attitude, pride, and basic messiness, love the truth of their life more than they love God. Therefore, that personal truth that which they hold on to so dearly then becomes their personal darkness. However, when we strive to walk in the light, we are willfully engaged in a personal walk with God. Notice I said striving to walk in the light! The Bible says everyone sins and falls short of God's glory. (Romans 3:23) Therefore, we need Jesus and His beautiful blood to cover us. This does not give us the right to walk any kind of way or the right to walk over others, but it does remind us that we will have moments when we fall during the walk. Being in the right fellowship with God first starts with right relationship, so then a right relationship with God opens the door to repentance. True repentance acknowledges our willful walk in the dark with a willful turn to a walk in the light. As we walk according to what pleases God, we have right relationship and right fellowship with God and others because the blood of Jesus cleanses us from all sin.

God desires for our walk to be authentic. A false fellowship has its roots in serving self instead of serving God. However, true fellowship with God leads to absolute surrender to God that implodes self-will for God's will. Many people avoid this true fellowship because there is accountability for our personal actions, and we have to be willing to put in the work. This is not a work that we are able to do alone. We need the Holy Spirit to help us. However, as God intervenes and helps us, we see parts of ourselves that we must change in an effort to obtain personal spiritual growth. Although change can be good, it still requires each person to be able to say "NO" to the self. This is not always the easiest thing to do. So, again we need God's help through this personal journey of fellowship. Another thing to recognize is when we desire to allow God to work on us and reveal to us internal issues that prevent us from conquering the Mountain called ME, we may feel the uncomfortable growing pangs of spiritual growth. As God begins to shatter pieces of us that are not needed, we have a tendency to try to hold on to the stuff that we don't need. So, then we have to take on the "LET IT GO" mindset! If it does not line us with the Word of God and His concepts and precepts, we need to LET IT GO!

As we master letting go of the things that are not valuable during our climb of Mountain ME and we become wise enough to acknowledge the need to stop being against self, then we begin the S T R E T C H. Our personal stretch to all that God desires for us to become is a never ending journey because He is the potter and we are the clay. He always is able to see if we need to be re-designed or re-purposed.

Jeremiah 18:4 reads, "But the vessel he was working on with the clay was ruined in the potter's hand. So, he remade it into another vessel that seemed appropriate to him..." we cannot be afraid of God's re-design for our lives. We also must not be afraid of what Gods says is appropriate use for us. A great example is the usher at church. You love the work of the usher. They look so handsome and beautiful in their uniforms. They smile at everyone, and they are so kind as they show the people to their seats. However, God knows that you have corns and bunions. God also knows that there's only a matter of time before someone steps on your feet and even though it may be an accident, you are not as polite as God would have you to be because

He is still working on you. Therefore, God thinks a better position for you would be the clerk behind the desk in the church bookstore. God knows this is a better placement for you, because you are an avid reader and you like to refer great books to others. The point is that God knows what is an appropriate use for us as Kingdom builders. Placing our trust in Him can be a little unsettling at first because as human beings we have a tendency to rely on our own understanding. However, there is another Scripture that is clear in its command,

"Trust in the Lord with all our hearts and lean not on our own understanding but in all our ways acknowledge Him, and He shall direct our path..." (Proverbs 3:5-6) When we place our trust in God, He shows us that path that helps others as well as ourselves. The role of the Holy Spirit at work in all of us is to help and not hurt. One of my Fathers in ministry, Arch Bishop Kelsey, invited my husband and I to get rubber bands and pass them out during worship. We did it and God began to speak to me about this rubber band. God revealed that sometimes the personal stretch feels just like a rubber band that is about to snap. You can feel the tension of the rubber band as you keep stretching it. However, because it was created to be stretched it does not snap, and it can be used for multiple assignments. As God stretches us beyond what we see as ruined, we can be re-designed or re-purposed to do other things that are important, appropriate, and valuable to God. Therefore, it is important to accept the personal stretch so that our trust and faith can be stretched just like the rubber band.

When we allow God to really stretch us, we develop a deeper faith and trust in God.

This exploration of our first climb: OVERCOME THE SELF TO SERVE GOD, reminds us to make the right decision and feed what we want to lead our lives. And if we desire the Holy Spirit to lead our lives, we need to become open to God's desires and to accept the things we must overcome. We need to stop being against ourselves, avoid false fellowship, and accept the personal stretch. These efforts will prepare us to climb to higher levels as we overcome the self to serve God.

CONQUERING THE MOUNTAIN CALLED ME

Name three self-sabotaging issues that you want to overcome?

What are some decisions that you need to make with God's help to become better? Are you ready to accept your personal stretch?

SHARON C. B. HUNTER

NOTES

CHAPTER 3
Follow God's Ordered Steps

Psalm 37:23 "...The steps of a *good* man are ordered by the LORD: and he delighteth in his way..."

When we decide to overcome the self in an effort to serve God, we begin to surrender all to Jesus. It is this surrender that encourages each person to follow the steps ordered by God. The Scripture puts it like this "...The steps of a *good* man are ordered by the LORD: and he delighteth in his way..." The first thing that we must acknowledge is the type of man or woman who is ordered by God. Some Bible versions say good man others say righteous man. However, the key is understanding that good or righteous breaks down to a person in the right relationship with God. Being in the right relationship with God means, we have taken the necessary steps to put away selfish behaviors that deter us from God's way of doing things. A right relationship with God does not mean that we are right in everything we do. However, it does mean that we serve a God that is perfect in everything that He does and have made the choice to follow this perfect God. So, then the second thing we must see in this text is the word STEPS. This implies even a good man or woman goes through a process when they follow God. Otherwise, there would not be a need to say "STEPS". So, then we may take 1, 2, 3 steps or for some of us we may have to continue to steps 4,5,6,7 etc. The point is that God knows what steps He has ordered for each of our journeys.

CONQUERING THE MOUNTAIN CALLED ME

We bump into problems on this journey up the Mountain ME because of the way we feel. The problem is our feelings can become complex and confusing. Our feelings can change. Our feelings can be buried deep in our heart. Our feelings can be removed and we can become seemingly emotionless so, in essence our feelings cannot be trusted. Therefore, following our feelings instead of following God's ordered steps will often lead us into deep ditches. So, the question may be asked, how then do we avoid this infamous ditch digging? The biggest battle between following God's ordered steps versus ditch digging is failing to seek God for direction. So, what does seeking God's face really mean? Well, in its simplest explanation, we should ask God for direction before we step out. This does not have to be an elaborate prayer but a simple acknowledgement to God that we don't know what we are doing, and that we need Him to lead and direct us. The second explanation in what does it mean to seek God's face is, wait for the answer! We often become restless in our own spirit when we have to wait. We become even more agitated if God begins to lead us some place we do not want to go. And typically where God is leading, does not fit into our own personal plan. So we reject God's plan. However, if we learn to seek God's face the Scripture says, "I know the plans I have for you declares the Lord, plans for welfare and not for calamity to give you a future and a hope..." (Jeremiah 29:11) I love this text because the children of Israel, like many of us, had made yet another decision to follow their own way. This is called apostasy. It took them down a path that led to 70 years of captivity. The situation was bleak and they felt hopeless, and God reminded them that the situation was not going away for a long while. However, even in their choices to do it their own way, God did not leave them alone. He reminded them He still had a plan. God has a way of giving the ease that we need to follow after Him. When we walk by faith and not by sight, we have the courage to reject our partial plans and do things God's way. God helps us know that He has a plan to give us a hope and a future.

So let's be honest, accepting that the plan you may have developed for your life a million moons ago is failing or has failed can be hard to stomach. Not because of God but because you have to get past what you wanted and accept that what God wants is better. This does not mean that God expects us to just be mindless people. As a matter of fact the Scriptures say, "... This day I call the heavens and the earth as witnesses against you that I have set before you life and death, blessings and curses. Now choose life, so that you and your children may live..." God presents us with the answer, 'choose life', but He still gives us a mind to choose! Here is a great example of why we should trust God's answer. In Louisville, KY each year we celebrate the Derby. It's a weeklong celebration of different events. One of the events is the Pegasus Parade. The parade starts on the east end of Broadway, a major thoroughfare. It travels about 3 or 4 miles headed to West Louisville. I remember a preacher from my old church used a parade to explain God's vision versus our vision, and

CONQUERING THE MOUNTAIN CALLED ME

I never forgot it! Rev. Carter said, we are only able to see the portion of the parade right in front of the section we sit. However, God is able to see the entire parade from start to finish. Our lives are much like the parade. We only can handle the present portion of our lives. However, God is able to see everything all at once. He is able to help us if we follow His ordered steps, choose life, and trust Him. However, in the final analysis, we choose.

Another thought to remember about following God's ordered steps is that each person is not given the same steps to follow. Each of us is given the same mission called, "The Great Commission." Matthew 28:18 "...And Jesus came and spoke unto them, saying, All power is given unto me in heaven and in earth. Mat 28:19 Go ye therefore, and teach all nations, baptizing them in the name of the Father, and of the Son, and of the Holy Ghost: Mat 28:20 Teaching them to observe all things whatsoever I have commanded you: and, lo, I am with you always, even unto the end of the world. Amen."

This is the Great Commission and this is the mission for every born again Christian. However, the method God gives each of us is different. This is why it is essential not to get caught up in what our brothers and sisters are doing. We have to trust God's ordered steps and follow our own path. We are able to derive from John 17 that Jesus calls us to be in the world but not of the world. Therefore, it is our job to come to Jesus to get better and go back and rescue our friends and family from the hateful second death with the help of the Holy Spirit. Now, with that being said, we all do not live the same lives. So then the method God uses is different for all of us because we all have not fallen in the same pits. But once we are saved and have made the decision to follow Jesus' ordered steps then we are able to reach back and help those who may have followed a similar destructive path. So again each of us has lived different lives therefore God then uses different methods to help those who want help.

As we learn to look to God to help us become the best person we can become, we have to understand it is an uphill journey. If you know anything about an uphill journey, it is work. We have to make the decision to stick with God, because we can't make the climb without Him. We have to understand the struggle with self is one that will never go away because we always want what we want. But if we trust God to lead us to the right steps and remain committed to those Godly steps, we will begin the necessary steps to conquer self, one day at a time.

The last thought to think about as we follow God's ordered steps is to study God's Word. The Word of God says,

(2Timothy 2:15) "...Study to show yourself approved to God, a workman that needs not to be ashamed, rightly dividing the word of truth..."

Often we walk a path and as we go we gain the approval of people. Although we may have not started off with the mind to please people, we have to be careful to continue to stay on the path that obtains God's approval versus the people. As we follow God, it should be our goal to understand His Word and God's plan to use His Word to help us and others. As we study to show ourselves approved to God, we begin to practice a great Christian concept that encourages God's people to place our focus and adoration on God. If we spend all our time seeking to please people, we will never follow the steps God has ordered for our lives. Simply because we are focusing on what the people think. And finally as we study the Word of God, we learn how to be a workman for God who uses God's Word correctly. So many times people will say they are following God's steps or hearing from God but they are not rightly dividing the Word of truth. They may have read the Word of God but they have not studied the Word of God and this error leads to taking God's Word out of context. So when we study God's Word it is to gain His approval and avoid twisting the Word of God to fit and justify the steps that we want to take. Because again in order to conquer self-serving habits so that we can become our best self, we must decide, commit, and follow God's ordered steps.

CONQUERING THE MOUNTAIN CALLED ME

Complete a 30 day plan that helps you make a greater commitment to God and following His steps.

NOTES

CHAPTER 4

No Man or Woman Is an Island

Ecclesiastes 4:12 "And if one prevails against him, two shall withstand him; and a threefold cord is not quickly broken..."

We are bombarded with slogans, mottos, idioms and old adages that attempt to summarize a thought or way of community. Some of them are very easy to understand while others are a little harder to wrap our minds around. However, I have a few that are my favorites. An African old adage that we hear a lot is, "It takes a village......" Another great idiom is "the icing on the cake". However, one of my all-time favorites today but totally confusing as a young woman growing in the Lord is, "No Man Is an Island"

I think the reason it was so confusing as a young woman was because to me, the saying made no sense. I looked at exactly what was being said and became confused. What was more confusing was that I heard people say this to me several times before I realized that they were talking about me. They were trying to tell me in a sugar-coated way, 'you can't live your life isolated from others.'

This thought was first introduced by poet John Donne who was interested in exploring the connectedness of people. As it pertains to the Bible, Mr. Donne was on to something. He penned the poem, "No Man is an Island" which reminds the reader that our lives are all intertwined with each other. The poem is not one that rhymes however, near the end he writes, "...for whom the bell tolls; it tolls for thee." Many years ago churches used to ring a bell when someone died. So, again another point he pushes is to encourage the readers that we should care because our lives are intertwined and connected.

So, understanding the thought fully is to accept the idea that we can't thrive alone. We need each other. Years later a Christian writer, Hezekiah Walker, penned the song, "I Need You to Survive"

Ecclesiastes 4:12 reads, "And if one prevail against him, two shall withstand him; and a threefold cord is not quickly broken..." We have to cooperate with one another. We can't live our lives isolating ourselves from others because we have been hurt so many times that we now trust no one. We are here to spread the Good News about Jesus Christ and this takes team work. The seventy were sent out in two's to expose others to the Gospel. If we view our lives like an island and are unable to function with others, then we run the risk of being overpowered. However, two people can defend themselves and a cord of three strands or three people cannot be easily broken.

The problem is, if you are so guarded then you will never receive anyone who would be willing to labor with you, love you, or even help you. Often these island behaviors surface after some type of hurt that leaves us guarded. The goal is not to tell everyone everything. However, it is to encourage us that living a life that is guarded all the time limits your learning. There is another poem with an unknown author. It is penned with the title, "Reason, Season, Lifetime." The entire poem has a deep teaching that shares that some people are in your life for a reason or a moment and then they are gone. While others are in your life for a season to help you learn something you may have never known. And lastly there are those who are there a lifetime and they teach you lifelong lessons to build upon. However, if you are living your life on an emotional or spiritual island you will never be able to tell the difference between people who are there for a reason, season, or lifetime. Who did God send to help you through the hard place? Who did God send to help you through a bad situation? Who did God send to help you a lifetime? These are the questions that can be answered if we are willing to live with a heart open to who God sends.

Another thing to remember after you have made the decision to allow someone in your life is that people will always be people! That means that they may say or do something to hurt you or your feelings. This is not always intentional but sometimes it is. However, the key is understanding that Jesus is perfection, and people are imperfect. So, then if you are hurt after you let your guard down, don't approach life going forward with the attitude, 'see I told you, can't trust nobody,' and revert back to island living again!

I think back and I thank God for people whom He wanted me to welcome in my life. I was not open to the idea at first. However, it took God to help me understand that this person not only was here to stay, but that they were one of my lifetime people. When God sends you a person who loves Him and studies His Word, you are able to learn if you open your heart. Remember the operating phrase is, 'when God sends you.' We should live our lives open to the people who God will send our way to help us along the way. Accepting someone in your life who has lived through something or who has a wisdom or knowledge that you do not possess does not mean that you are weak, dumb, or useless. It means that you are a wise person to recognize that God has sent someone to help and you are humble enough to accept that help.

Climbing the mountain called me will require us to accept help from others. We will need to follow the Holy Spirit to know who He will send to help us. We cannot dictate to God who He desires to send to help us for a reason, season or lifetime. So, remember, stop living life like an island. Open your heart to Jesus and the Holy Spirit who will lead you to the people whom He intends to send.

Are you ready to accept God's help how God send's His help?

CONQUERING THE MOUNTAIN CALLED ME

Notes

SHARON C. B. HUNTER

CHAPTER 5
Follow GPS-God's Positioning System

Luke 22:42 Saying, "Father, if You are willing, remove this cup from me, yet not my will, but Yours be done."

Several years ago, I drove to Indianapolis, Indiana to help handle some church business. The first Lady of the church and several other ladies traveled as well. One of the ladies took it upon herself to get her brothers G.P.S. system. Basically, all we had to do was follow the directions that GPS was giving us. Now the truth was that I had driven to Indianapolis what seems like a thousand times so, it would have been easy to travel my own way. However, the problem with that choice was that when I got to the places during the journey that were unfamiliar, I would have become lost, confused, and irritated. So, I chose to obey the G.P.S. directions. However, it made me think about the many times in my life when I did not follow God's Word. He gave us the Bible to lead us through life and all its hard places. The Bible functions just like a GPS. As a matter of fact, we can call the Bible **G**od's **P**ositioning **S**ystem. Yahweh gave us His Word to be our personal G.P.S. system yet when we do things our way, we become lost, confused, and irritated. God wants to bless each of us outside of anything that we could ask or think to ask, but we must OBEY!

The entire goal behind any GPS system is that you find your destination without getting lost. So, then if we decide not to follow God's

CONQUERING THE MOUNTAIN CALLED ME

Positioning System, then we will find ourselves in perplexing situations. When we set out to conquer the mountain called me, we must learn to accept and follow God's direction. This means that there may be moments when we want to go in a specific direction but God is directing us in an altogether different direction. Let me give you a great example. I was on my morning walk. I came out of the house, locked my door, and proceeded to walk down the sidewalk. As I got to the stop sign at the end of my street, I wanted to go my regular route. However, I felt the spirit of the Lord leading me to go in a different direction. I stood there at the crossroads unable to decide. Should I go the way that is familiar or take the less familiar route with God leading the way? Even though I wrestled with the decision there was no need to wrestle. God's direction is always better but because I was still wrestling with my direction, I didn't hear anything from God. As I stood there for what seemed like forever, God dropped some understanding on my spirit. He allowed me to understand in that moment that He had already given me the right direction and it was not necessary to repeat it. However, it was necessary for me to obey. We have to understand that our relationship with God is not like those with our regular friends. Don't get me wrong, the Word of God says in John 15:15 that he no longer calls us servants but friends. So, if God is all things good and out of that goodness we are given love, friendship, and the right instructions, then it is our Christian responsibility to follow Him. He deserves our respect. The sad reality is that we don't always do as we are told. We often get to the crossroads of life and are given the correct path to follow yet we do what we want, and typically we suffer for it.

God's Word is a simple compass that navigates us through life's complexities. However, it is also a compass to position us in the purpose God has for our lives and catapult us to our destiny. Often when we hear the word position our minds may gravitate to money, titles, and power. However, God understands that life is saturated with trouble and triumph. So then His desire is to position us to be able to experience Godly balance. A great example comes from my teen years. I was a basketball player and one of the plays our coach, Tena Leahy, taught was the pick and roll. You had to hustle down court find your spot behind your opponent and position your feet. My teammate would handle the ball to the left or right side of the court. The opponent would follow my teammate but when the opponent would turn to follow the ball she would run right into the teammate that was still planted and in position, and we would score! When we look at our lives our destiny is the score! God wants to see us win, but we have to be willing to obey God's instruction and stay in position. Another thing to know about position is that the flesh will try to push us out of position. What I mean is we will be tempted to follow our flesh and be led out of position. However, the smart thing to do is to stick with God until He says move. No matter how uncomfortable, no matter how silly we feel, no matter how good it may look to move before instruction, do not move until God says move and you will score! So then another aspect of positon is timing. God knows the exact time to bring us up and move us forward. However, it still requires an obedience and allegiance to God's will and way.

The Bible serves as God's Positioning System as we travel through life. It is important to acknowledge that God's Word holds our master plan that will not fail. The unfortunate reality is that we fail. We fail to trust God's master plan. We fail to open our minds and hearts to God. We fail to wait and watch God work. Therefore we always end up with the short end of the stick. This predicament has nothing to do with God but everything to do with our personal decisions.

Bad decisions lead you straight to "The land of Through." However, keeping the Bible close to your heart and using it as a positioning system will help each of us navigate the land of "Through." So then, the wise thing to do would be to first, accept that life will always take you "Through," but if we use the proper navigation system then we will reach God's divine destiny much faster.

Let's look at examples. You have made the bad choice of chasing the money versus seeking the plan that God has for your life and the decision is now choking the life out of you. God presents a way of escape which requires you to position yourself in more faith but less money. However, the enemy presents a job with even more money but it compromises your integrity. What is the best choice? Here is the answer, if God is in the presentation of the direction to go, always bank on God! Yes, sometimes the money may not be where you want it to be but if your faith is increased and you are on a new level with God the climb is worth it.

Here is another example, you have great love for family and you live for God. You make decisions that honor God. You have spent years praying for others in their time of need and have watched God bring them THROUGH. However, your family member becomes deathly ill and you pray to God in confidence to spare your family member. He has another idea that did not line up with your request. Do you listen to Satan and receive, accept, and digest His lies about God? Or do you rejoice and trust in God's complete omniscient ability? The altimeter is a small handheld GPS system that helps mountain climbers reach their destinations. As born again believers, God's Word is our altimeter. It helps us reach life's toughest destinations. Even Jesus experienced moments when He wanted to follow His own way. He said, "Father, if You are willing, remove this cup from Me..." His statement started with Him asking God the Father for another direction. However, His heart and mind were settled on following God so, His response was, "not my will but thy will..." So, the lesson to learn from Jesus is following God's Word or **G**od's **P**ositioning **S**ystem will always challenge us, but His Word will never fail us. His Word will always help us avoid the sludge of SHOUDA', COULDA', AND WOULDA'!

How have you allowed God to re-direct you in the midst of frustrating moments?

CONQUERING THE MOUNTAIN CALLED ME

Think about how this made you feel and write a brief explanation.

NOTES

CHAPTER 6
AVOIDING THE SLUDGE OF COULDA', SHOULDA', AND WOULDA'

James 1:5-8 "If any of you lacks wisdom, you should ask God, who gives generously to all without finding fault, and it will be given to you. But when you ask, you must believe and not doubt, because to the one who doubts is like a wave of the sea, blown and tossed by the wind. That person should not expect to receive anything from the Lord. Such a person is double-minded and unstable in all they do."

Wouldn't it be nice every time we had to make a decision that God would send a big neon sign that says, "Go this way!"

Don't get me wrong God is faithful to lead us, but as discussed before, we can get in our own way. Overcoming the self is a life-long process, and during this process we can mess up! These mess ups create a pit of despair and at the bottom of that pit is the sludge of COULDA', SHOULDA', AND WOULDA'. We didn't notice it before because we were engaged in accomplishing what we set out to do but after one or two failures, we begin to slip on the sludge of COULDA', SHOULDA', AND WOULDA'. Climbing the mountain called ME is virtually impossible if we are only focused on getting out of pits of despair which is what is behind us versus the climb ahead of us.

Let us first get an understanding of what sludge is. It is mud and mire. It is a mixture of thick, soft, wet mud or a viscous mixture of liquid and solid components. When you attempt to navigate through sludge, the pressure of the muck and mire creates a sucking factor. As you try to walk through it, you can feel the pressure sucking your feet and holding you in one spot.

In my head I see COULDA', SHOULDA', AND WOULDA' as a three headed sludge spitting dragon. It is ugly and anything with three heads is freaky! And most importantly, it hinders the climb of Mountain ME.

Coulda': <u>Overwhelmed with options</u>. James 1:5 "*If any of you lacks wisdom, you should ask God, who gives generously to all without finding fault, and it will be given to you.*"

Let's start with COULDA'. It is always great to have options because options present choices. We choose if we like the red one or the blue one. We decide if we want to go to the Bahamas or Myrtle Beach. However, sometimes the decisions that we make go sideways and, everything seems to fall apart. When this happens, we find FAULT with our decision and begin to consider all the things we COULD HAVE DONE BETTER.

I could have married a better man or woman. I could have gone to a better school. I could have started a better business. The COULDA' head of the sludge dragon comes out when we think we COULD have taken advantage of better options that were available at the time.

The COULDA' head of the sludge dragon is there to confuse, frustrate, and tempt us to lean in on our own UNDERSTANDING even though the Word of God states, to LEAN NOT ON YOUR OWN UNDERSTANDING.(Proverbs 3:5-7)

How can we climb the Mountain called ME if we are constantly looking back to what we could have done. The higher we climb the Mountain ME, the more difficult it becomes to keep using all our tools to climb upwards, yet we are looking backwards. It is dangerous and ineffective.

Shoulda': Second guessing decisions.

It does not take long for the second head of the Sludge dragon to surface called SHOULDA' because when we begin to think of the things we COULD HAVE done, it leads us to the things WE THINK of what we SHOULD HAVE DONE. I should have waited. I should have moved. I should have taken this job. I should have married this person, I should have-- you fill in the blank.

The function of the SHOULDA' head of this freaky dragon is to temp us to walk in double-mindedness and function out of unstableness.

The Bible records in James 1:6 *"...But when you ask, you must believe and not doubt, because the one who doubts is like a wave of the sea, blown and tossed by the wind. That person should not expect to receive anything from the Lord. Such a person is double-minded and unstable in all they do...."*

As you climb a real mountain, you can't spend time second guessing every step you take to climb higher. This unstable thought process increases your chances of falling off the mountain. It is the same as you climb Mountain ME. If you continue to second guess every thought, you cannot function in stability. And this instability continues to follow you in everything you do.

Woulda': Excuses and The Blame game

Then there is the WOULDA' head of the dragon. This is the vicious game of blaming others for your failures. I would have married someone who was better for me if people would have stopped pushing me to marry. I would have gone to a better school if my family would have had more money or, I would not have turned out like this if God loved me like He loves others.

This one to me is the most vicious because it puts you against all those who love you most, God, family and friends. Mankind has this gene in us. Most people know the Bible story of Adam and Eve. When the deed was done,

God came walking through the garden in the cool of day. Adam and Eve were hiding from God. The Lord called to Adam, "Where are you?" Adam answers, "I heard you in the garden, and I was afraid because I was naked so, I hid." God responds, "Who told you that you were naked? Have you eaten from the tree that I commanded you not to eat from?"

This is the part of the story that I always find interesting because we see the head of the WOULDA' dragon revealed in Scripture. Adam does not take responsibility for his actions. He blames God and the woman. As a matter of fact, he responds, "The woman you put here with me, she gave me some fruit from the tree and I ate it." However, when God turns to the woman and says, "What is this you have done?" The woman, Eve answers, "The serpent deceived me, and I ate..." So, the husband blamed God and the wife, and the wife blamed the serpent.

People start playing the blame game when they don't want to be responsible for their failure.

I have said it so many times before and even wrote about it in my last book, *"Suddenly Saved, Single and Parenting."* There is favor in the failure.

However, if we waste all our time in the sludge of COULDA', SHOULDA', WOULDA' then we miss the favor of failure.

Like any dragon or beast, it can be easily taken down with the help of God. So, let's look at ways to avoid the sludge of the COULDA', SHOULDA', WOULDA' dragon and take down this nasty beast

The first thing we can do to overcome all of the COULDA's is explore the praise, prayer and thanks.

1 Thessalonians 5:16-18 says, "...Rejoice always, pray without ceasing, give thanks in all circumstances; for this is the will of God in Christ Jesus for you..."

No matter what life throws our way, we should do what the Word says and that is rejoice always. Give Thanks in all Circumstances—Psalms 34 puts it like this I will bless the Lord at all times. His praise shall continuously be in my mouth... Life will always have moments when things go sideways. However, whatever the circumstance KEEP PRAISING, DON'T DOUBT, and DON'T COMPLAIN OR

CONQUERING THE MOUNTAIN CALLED ME

BLAME because it is God's will that we Bless His name in all situations.

We also should pray without ceasing which means develop a consistent prayer life. We do not have to keep praying for the same thing like we don't believe God can do it. However, we can allow God to develop in us a consistent prayer time and life with Him.

When we spend time in prayer asking for God's guidance, He is faithful to give us direction. Therefore, we recognize all of the options that are available but the difference is that we have confidence that God has led us in the right direction. So, then we do not have to agonize over all the options if something seems to go wrong. If God leads us in any given direction, then it cannot go wrong. Now, remember there is no guarantee that how God works something out for you will be what you saw in your head. As a matter of fact, God usually works things out much differently than what we expected but we know that WHEN WE HAVE PRAISED, PRAYED, AND THANKED GOD THEN, HE IS FAITHFUL TO GIVE US WISDOM GENEROUSLY TO HELP US.

Another important thing to remember is the simplicity of receiving God's wisdom. It is as easy as asking God for it.

The Bibles says in James 1:5 *"...If any of you lacks wisdom, you should ask God, who gives generously to all without finding fault, and it will be given to you..."* So, then The Word of God says all we have to do is ASK for wisdom and God GIVES it generously. God does not want us to be unstable and double-minded. So, temptation pushes us to consider something we SHOULDA' done, but God wants us to simply ask for wisdom, receive what He generously gives, and stop talking about the past.

He is not the kind of God who looks to FIND FAULT in past poor choices. He is the quintessential teacher.

The last point: Never indulge in the blame game. Whatever problems develop, own them! Don't blame God, family, self, or friends. Just own the fact that you are not in an ideal situation and you had something to do with it. However, don't lose sight of the FACT that FAITH in God can turn everything around!

We know that faith is the substance of things hoped for and the evidence not seen,

(Hebrews 11:1) but the portion of this text that I love is Hebrews 11:6 The Bible says in Hebrews 11:6 says, *"...But without faith it is impossible to please him: for he that cometh to God must believe that he is, and that he is a rewarder of them that diligently seek him..."*

Jesus never asks us to do anything that He Himself has not done first. So, then Jesus had FAITH in God and approached Him, truthfully. When Jesus approached God in prayer in the Garden of Gethsemane, His mind could have been rocking and reeling about all the things He COULDA' done. However, His Faith was STRONG and MIGHTY. He asked for what he wanted "...if there is a way for this cup to pass..."

CONQUERING THE MOUNTAIN CALLED ME

BUT He did not let His FEELINGS override His FAITH in God. So, then he said, '...not my will but thy will be done...'

Many of us are learning how to put our FEELINGS aside and FUNCTION out of our FAITH in God.

How many people want to please God? Therefore, we have to RECEIVE GOD'S WISDOM and lay aside all of our COULDA'S, SHOULDA'S, AND WOULDA'S and allow God to strengthen our FAITH.

When we approach God we have to KNOW that HE IS who? GOD!

As Jesus hung between two thieves that day, He could have been focused on the CSW (Coulda's, Shoulda's, and Woulda's) but He prayed for family, friends, and enemies. Even though it looked like His situation had gone sideways, He STILL sought God. The Word says that God IS rewarding of those who DILEGENTLY SEEK HIM. So, God is not just giving out the reward but He rewards those who do something, DILEGENTLY SEEK HIM!

How do we DILEGENTLY SEEK God? Diligence is a consistent, constant effort to accomplish whatever is undertaken.

We have to be willing to:

1. To search for God

2. To investigate His Word

3. To hunger for More of Him

Remember, God has a reward for those who diligently seek Him. However, for those who TRUST their feelings versus their FAITH in God, for those who agonize over self-driven decisions, TRY SOMETHING NEW IN GOD and leave behind all the COULD HAVE, SHOULD HAVE, AND WOULD HAVE'S and Master the Faith that God has made available to you. Not only will this allow us to avoid the sludge of coulda', shoulda', and woulda' but it will help us get back up when we fail at conquering the mountain called ME.

Are you willing to "put in the work" to search for God?

Name 5 things you have learned from investigating God's Word

What does it mean to hunger for God?

NOTES

CHAPTER 7
GET OVER IT!

Philippians 4:8 Finally, brothers, whatever is true, whatever is honorable, whatever is fair, whatever is pure, whatever is acceptable, whatever is commendable, if there is anything of excellence and if there is anything praiseworthy—keep thinking about these things.

Philippians 4:9 Likewise, keep practicing these things: what you have learned, received, heard, and seen in me. Then the God of peace will be with you...

The word conquer is defined: To successfully overcome; to gain control of (a problem or weakness) through great effort or to gain mastery over or win by overcoming obstacles or opposition

<Conquered the mountain>

When you hear the word conquer and even look at the definition it may leave you with the impression that whatever the issue, it is over and done once conquered. Although, I agree with this thought, I also understand that in life we have problems and weaknesses that surface in multiple areas. Therefore, it is highly likely that we can overcome one problem or weakness and then have other problems or weaknesses that need attention. So, then if we are truly looking to conquer the mountain called me, we have to invest our time, talent and treasure into a source that is able to help us overcome and master obstacles as they present themselves throughout our lives. The Word of God promises that Jesus has come that we might have life, and that they might have *it* (life) more abundantly. Part of the reason that many of us live in lack is that we have failed to use the BIBLE as the resource to help us overcome useless actions, habits, and emotions. The goal of this book is to introduce concepts and precepts found in the Bible that will help each of us and our families GET OVER IT! So, the BIBLE is the **BA**SIC **I**NSTRUCTION **BE**FORE **LE**AVING **E**ARTH, which is the acronym for the Bible, and it will open up life more abundantly. The Bible can teach us how to GET OVER IT! Now, remember IT is like a chameleon. IT changes from person to person. IT will be conquered then re-surface as something totally different. No matter the case all the ITS require help from the Word of God. Getting over IT and getting to the truth can be quick in human years, or really long in those same human years. However, whatever the case, the Bible is THE TRUTH and it has an answer for everybody's IT. You may be sitting there thinking, 'well, if the Bible is the best answer then why don't all people turn to the Bible?' I would say this is an excellent question. The answer is, human beings don't always like the truth nor do we respond to the truth as truth and change. When we set out to conquer the Mountain called ME the only spike that digs into the Mountain of ME so that we can climb to higher personal heights is the Bible. As we develop as Christians we will learn things that are true, honorable, fair, pure, acceptable, and even commendable.

CONQUERING THE MOUNTAIN CALLED ME

Typically these are things that people categorize as excellent and yes, even praiseworthy. The Bible says, in Philippians 4:8, "think on these things". Often we think on the things that upset us. We agonize over the things that happened in our past. We focus on what we want and how we want it. We hang on to the hurts of yesterday and the fears of tomorrow. However, God releases in His Word the ability to trust in Him. For that reason, we can take the Word at its word! We should think on these good things and then practice them as we live.

A great athlete becomes great because he has mastered the concept that practice is a daily activity. Therefore, the thing he learns from his coaches and others he receives and puts into action. Philippians 4:8 reminds us that we have to put into practice the things we have learned from God's Word every day. I like to be truthful, therefore practicing the Word of God can be a challenge. Not because God makes it hard or He enjoys seeing us struggle. Practicing the Word of God becomes difficult because of our flesh. It gets in the way of what the Word says is right. Instead of practicing what the Word of God commands, we end up practicing what feels good to our flesh. This lesser mountain of selfish efforts was never meant to be conquered because it benefits no one including ourselves. It simply encourages a person to stay stuck in self-absorbed activities. Therefore, they never learn how to GET OVER IT.

Again, I like to be truthful. It is possible to GET OVER IT and there are steps we need to take. However, today we are going to look at three steps that are imperative! The first step in getting over any issue and getting on with your life is deciding that you want to be done with IT. It is as simple as that. I am ready to be done. When we enter into this frame of mind, nobody can change our mind because we want to be done. We have made a decision. It is our choice.

The second step in getting over any life issue once you decide you are ready to be done is to move away from people, places, and situations that drag you down or suck the life out of you. After we move away from our messy decisions of the past, we must move toward God to get to our Godly destinations. Getting over it and moving toward God, introduces us to the righteousness of God. Becoming a righteous man or woman of God, does not mean that you are right in every choice you have ever made. However, it does mean you are in right relationship with God. Having a right relationship with God puts you in tune with the Spirit of God and His direction.

The third step in getting over any matter once we have made the decision to be done, we are ready to move away from messy situations and move toward God , then we have to get in tune with God. As we have learned how to put God's Word into full effect through practice, God will lead us to leadership that has submitted to God's will. We are safe to follow the Christ Jesus we see in those that follow him. God has a way of speaking through people so that others may learn and continue to teach others about Jesus. However, the last verse of Philippians 4:9 is, "...*Then the God of peace will be with you.*"

CONQUERING THE MOUNTAIN CALLED ME

God does not treat us like unwanted children. He takes interest in our efforts and promises to be with us. This is an amazing truth found in the Word of God in more than once place:

Deuteronomy 31:6, Be strong and courageous. Do not be afraid or terrified because of them, for the LORD your God goes with you; "He will never leave you nor forsake you."

Deuteronomy 31:8, The LORD himself goes before you and will be with you; He will never leave you nor forsake you. "Do not be afraid; do not be discouraged."

Joshua 1:5, No one will be able to stand up against you all the days of your life. "As I was with Moses, so I will be with you; I will never leave you nor forsake you."

1Kings 8:57, "May the LORD our God be with us as he was with our fathers; may He never leave us nor forsake us."

1Chronicles 28:20, David also said to Solomon his son, "Be strong and courageous, and do the work." Do not be afraid or discouraged, for the LORD God, my God is with you. He will not fail you or forsake you until all the work for the service of the temple of the LORD is finished."

Psalms 37:28, For the LORD loves the just and will not forsake his faithful ones. "They will be protected forever, but the offspring of the wicked will be cut off;"

Psalms 94:14 "For the LORD will not reject his people; he will never forsake his inheritance."

CONQUERING THE MOUNTAIN CALLED ME

Isaiah 41:17 "The poor and needy search for water, but there is none; their tongues are parched with thirst. But I the LORD will answer them; I, the God of Israel, will not forsake them."

Isaiah 42:16 "I will lead the blind by ways they have not known, along unfamiliar paths I will guide them; I will turn the darkness into light before them and make the rough places smooth. These are the things I will do; I will not forsake them."

Hebrew 13:5 Keep your lives free from the love of money and be content with what you have, because God has said, "Never will I leave you; never will I forsake you."

It is beautiful to know that as we set out on this quest to conquer the mountain ME, God is with us and He is committed to the journey of helping us GET OVER IT!

What issue have you had or still have that you are ready to make the decision to GET OVER IT?

CONQUERING THE MOUNTAIN CALLED ME

NOTES

SHARON C. B. HUNTER

CHAPTER 8
What makes us More Than Conquerors?

Romans 8:37 "Nay, in all these things we are more than conquerors through him that loved us."

I used to work for a fortune 500 company. One of their best practices was doing something one time and being done with that situation. I suppose in the business world issues rise up against a client's account and this practice is perfect. You never want a client calling in about the same thing over and over and over again. However, as we live our day to day lives we, prayerfully, will figure out that this is not an approach that will work. In my personal opinion, conquering the mountain called me is an ongoing climb of personal effectiveness. You and I will never be able to have a one and done approach to living and learning better choices. There will always be something that needs to be tweaked, changed, turned, and conquered. However, the key in Christian living is understanding what the Word of God says about conquerors. Romans 8:37 says, "Nay, in all these things we are more than conquerors through him that loved us."

What I love about this text is that it clearly states that we are more than conquerors.

The question is what makes us more than Conquerors? The first point in understanding how we are more than conquerors or how to become more than a conqueror is to BE REAL! One thing that upsets me in our present time is that we have so many people who do not know God, they do not know the word of God, they don't and refuse to understand the move of God YET have so much to say about a person's walk with God. So, since some Christians have bought that bill of goods related to the SUPER CHRISTIAN SYNDROME, they believe that Christians can do no wrong.

Now, beloved, that can go both ways. These folks may believe they can: Never say a bad word, never make a bad decision, always understand the move of God, always cross the "T's" and always, always, always dot the "I's." The opposite attitude is some people NEVER give God a chance to show them they can BECOME MORE than a conqueror.

Sadly enough, Christians and some potential Christians miss the move of God. They believe this messy message and live defeated lives because they refuse to just BE REAL!

If I never had a problem, then I would never KNOW that Jesus can fix it! The Scripture reminds us in Romans 8:37- *Nay, in all these things...* These are the HARDSHIPS or CONFLICTS people face when they BECOME MORE THAN a Conqueror.

Who lied and said we would never have a problem to conquer, or a hardship to face? Believers have always had to face hardships! These hardships manifest in many different ways:

1. Jesus faced Persecution and so do we.
2. Moses faced an impossible situation and so do we.
3. Joseph faced Imprisonment and so do we.

4. David faced Self-inflicted hardships as well as hardships inflicted by others and so do we
5. Jesus faced death and so do we.

However, we have to understand before we can move forward in this next realm of understanding the self we have to BE REAL. Nobody gets help if we are not real about how far God has brought us. One Sunday I was visiting a church and I was asked to sing after a visiting Pastor preached a powerful message. The Pastor preached. I sang, and the Pastor of the church exhorted, BUT GOD got the GLORY. When they called for people who had suffered with drug addiction to come to the altar, people started to pop up like popcorn. They were not afraid to be real and admit that this was once a problem that had conquered them but now they were more than conquerors because they had the victory.

The victory is what makes us more than conquerors. In order to be more than a conqueror, we had to have something that needed to be conquered. And I will say it again, if I never had a problem to face, I would never know that there was a Jesus who could fix it.

The second point to remember as we seek to understand how we are more than conquerors is to get delivered and stay delivered! Often we will overcome some issue in our lives but we make the decision to go back to the mess. The Word of God records it like this in Proverbs 26:11 *As a dog returns to his vomit, so a fool returns to his folly.* So, just like a dog, we go back to the mess and lick up whatever we have been delivered from. We are able to call on the great name of Jesus and GET DELIVERED and STAY DELIVERED. However, the truth is we have to be desperate and determined that we want our deliverance. WE MUST REPENT of our sin and spend some time praying and fasting. This is some WORK! I have even heard people call this HARDCORE CHRISTIANITY. Although I think it strange to call deliverance hardcore, what I will say is that we have to want to become an active participant in our own deliverance. Some people just want to take a pill for it or have a surgeon cut it away, but beloved, when we GET DELIVERENCE we have to be ACTIVE. WE HAVE to DO Something

One of my mentors says, "Salvation is free it's the maintenance that will cost you..."

I want you to read these next five facts about deliverance and remember that you are more than a conqueror:

Fact #1

Stick with the POWER SOURCE First Peter 5:8 warns us that our adversary is seeking whom he may devour. One of his primary targets is a believer who does not have the proper spiritual connection or covering in two areas:

**Leadership. God gave gifts (the fivefold ministry) to the church for the maturity of the saints (see Eph. 2:20). Leadership helps us not only mature but maintain the deliverance.

**Fellowship. God warns us not to forsake the assembling of ourselves together (see Heb. 10:24-25). Those who allow themselves to be separated from the flock, the enemy will devour.

FACT#2

Study the Word of God- We have to study the Word of God because it nourishes our spirit. The Word of God offers direction when we find ourselves at life's crossroads. The Word of God will give us every tool we need to be more than a conqueror as we conquer the Mountain called ME. I am certain there are many more in depth things to say about the Word of God. However, the main message will still be the same, study the Word of God.

FACT#3

Separate yourself When God has delivered you and you obtain victory in an area of your life, you must have an ear to hear further instructions from the Lord. God takes you from one level to the next, but there are new distractions on every level. So, we have to separate ourselves from the mess we once knew so we CAN HEAR GOD clearly for ourselves and others.

God replaces the group you lost with the body of Christ. So, again God warns us not to forsake the assembling of ourselves together.

FACT #4

SUBMIT YOURSELVES TO GOD -Jas 4:7 Therefore, submit yourselves to God. The definition of submit is to accept or yield to a superior force or to the authority or will of another person. It is safe to say when we submit ourselves to another there should be a level of trust for that person, superior force, or authority. Therefore submitting ourselves to God opens us up to trusting in Him but also resting in God and His will for our lives.

FACT #5

RESIST THE DEVIL James 4:7 Resist the devil, and he will run away from you.

I am certainly not going to tell you these are the only five things you can do. There are so many more things. However, these five will get you on the right track!

James 4:8 Come close to God, and he will come close to you. Cleanse your hands, you sinners, and purify your hearts, you double-minded.

I can't stress it enough, we have to become active participants in our own deliverance. Choose to submit to God. Choose to resist the devil. Choose to come closer to God.

Discuss five facts about deliverance

NOTES

CHAPTER 9
Conquer FEARS

Philippians 4:13 "..I can do all things through Christ Jesus who strengthens me..."

I will be very honest. I do not promise to know everything there is to know. However, the things I have learned as I have lived I do not mind sharing, and one thing I have learned in my living is being scared is a very human thing. The title of this book is *Conquering the mountain called ME* because it is our own personal issues, problems, and fears that hold us back from being and becoming the best Men or Women of God we can be. We get so side-tracked with fears that haven't happened yet we approach them as if they already have happened. We then choose not to take a leap of faith because of the fear that is holding us down like a bully on the playground. I will also share another issue that I have. I get upset with the Super-Christian who teaches we can never be hurt. We can never be angry. We can never be upset. We can never be sad. We can never be sick. We can never be afraid. These teachings are simply ludicrous. As human beings we were created in the image of God. Therefore, God, who Himself has emotion, states in **Isaiah 43:4**

"Since you are precious in My sight, since you are honored and *I love you*, I will give other men in your place and other peoples in exchange for your life. **Jeremiah 31:3** says, "...The LORD appeared to him from afar, saying, "I have *loved you with an everlasting love; Therefore I have drawn you with* *lovingkindness...*" **Exodus 22:24** says, "*My anger* will be kindled, and I will kill you with the sword, and your wives shall become widows and your children fatherless...." Matthew 9:36 says, "...Seeing the people, He felt compassion for them, because they were distressed and dispirited like sheep without a shepherd...." although there are many more, the last one we will use is, Matthew 20:34 "...Moved with compassion, Jesus touched their eyes; and immediately they regained their sight and followed Him..."

We must take heed of this knowledge and recognize that we are created in the image of God so we will have emotion. But there is a difference between having emotion and being emotional. When a person is emotional, they can be unstable and erratic in their behaviors. However God does not want us to have erratic or unstable behaviors. He has given us everything in His Word that will help us remain stable through the Word of God and clear minded.

However, the problems that surface and hold us are connected to emotional behaviors that can paralyze us. God wants us to keep moving with Him on our mind even when we feel fearful. 2 Timothy 1:7 says, "...For God has not given us the spirit of fear but of power, and of love; and of a sound mind..." This text encourages each believer that God did not give us a cowardly spirit. God gave us His spirit of power. We have the courage to overcome our fears and find a resolution to what is making us afraid if we continue to follow God. The word coward is a very strong word. However, when we become so afraid to move because of what might happen we become a coward. We have the power that will help us overcome obstacles, trials and dangers because the Word of God says, He gave us the power. However, not only does God expect us to use the power He has given us but He expects us to encourage others to let them know that they also have this same power of God. God also gave us His spirit of love. As we live our lives, there will always be moments when fear pours down to our feet like wet cement. It makes us feel like we cannot move. However, love reminds us that if we don't move something bad is going to happen. We see hero's and shero's running into the face of danger to save family, friends, and sometimes strangers because of the love of God and the power he has given them to cast aside the fear that wants to hold them. So, someone's life is changed forever because they accepted the power, love, and sound mind that God has given us all His believing children. Another thing to remember is that God has given us a sound mind. So, in clear conscience I want each person to know that once we have the tools to conquer our personal fears in one area, they will re-surface in another area. This is why it's important to remember how you overcame the very first fear, with the help of God. Therefore, when the enemy comes at us like a flood and attempts to hand-cuff us back to fear we are able to recite Scripture like: "...I can do all things through Christ Jesus who strengthens me..." or " I am more than a conqueror through Jesus Christ..." or "...with God all things are possible..." The key in unlocking each of these Scriptures for our lives is with God we can do it! Whatever IT

CONQUERING THE MOUNTAIN CALLED ME

is we can do it because we have decided to walk in God's spirit of power, love, and sound mind. Let's look at some fears to overcome so we can move forward for Christ.

What fears have you conquered?
What other fear re-surfaced?
What Scriptures have helped you unlock your mind to believe anything is possible?

NOTES

CHAPTER 10
Conquer the FEAR of Failure

"...lean not on your own understanding..."
Proverbs 3:5

I don't believe people get up every morning with the mind and heart that says, 'let's see how I can fail today.' However, if failure occurs, and it will, a better question to ask ourselves is what will I learn from this? And how do I get up from this failure? One of the greatest blessings a failure can teach us is that God grants favor in the failure because if we never try we will never know what will or won't work. If we never try we will never know what it feels like to re-think, re-group, and re-try. If we never try we will never understand the concept flop or fly!

We live in a society that places value on everything we do. If a student is in school the work is graded as A, B, C, D, or F. Whatever path is taken the student begins to understand the value of the work she or he have done. This is not a bad thing because we do need to have a gauge on how well we are doing and how much work needs to be done. However, it is equally important to spend time thinking about what we have learned from the failure. A great example is if you received a D as a grade you can ask yourself what you learned. When you are truthful to yourself, you will find out that you did not put forth the best effort. You did not study. You failed to do your part. However, you then have the choice to read more, study more, and put forth more effort. The effort must be intentional. We have to be intentional about our effort and our desire to learn from the failure. Once we extract what we are supposed to learn we can use that information when we try again.

Sometimes when people fail they take on the 'I have fallen and I can't get up' mindset. They see themselves in that fallen position without looking and learning how to get up from the situation. Our goal may be to never fail but life does not happen that way. Failure is a part of life but getting up is too. The favor God extends to all who receive His help creates an opportunity to re-think, re-group, and re-try. If life leads us to a place of failure, we have to re-think our steps so that we can discover the place where we went wrong. There is no need to re-invent the wheel so, if the first fifteen steps were good but it was step sixteen that caused the problem. Let us start at step sixteen! This then requires a re-group of thinking! We have to approach step sixteen differently because what we did the first time did not work. At this point, we should start reading, researching, praying and fasting. The word of God says, "...lean not on your own understanding..." (Proverbs 3:5) So, it is important to lean on God's Word and listen to what God has to say as we read, research, pray and fast. The re-try step is important because FEAR will begin to speak at this step in the juncture. Fear will say things to you like, 'who do you think you are?' or 'you should have never tried this in the first place.' There are many other voices that we hear in our ear that are FEAR speaking to discourage us. We have to put Jesus on this case of FEAR and allow Him to lead us to the right place. However, in order to receive that help we must re-try. We have to conquer our fear to fail and just re-try it! I remember several years back, God spoke in my spirit before I wrote my first book or delved deeper in ministry that FLOP OR FLY, YOU MUST TRY! In essence, God was encouraging me to try because the greater disservice to myself would be never to try. This would be the true FLOP because I never tried or re-tried. In conclusion, the point of this chapter is to remind us again that FEAR is a part of life. However, we can overcome the fear just by a simple try. We are able to conquer fear by remembering that if the fear never goes away we can learn ways to get around it so that we do not miss wonderful opportunities to grow, develop, and mature. Overcoming the mountain called ME will be fearful because it challenges us to confront the familiar and go for the Stretch! The familiar are the things that whether we receive them as good or bad experiences, we are familiar with them and their results but God wants to STRETCH us in our faith. However, this stretch cannot coexist with a paralyzing fear. We will conquer the fear of failure by pushing through the fear and accepting the help from God and receiving the favor in the failure to re-think, re-group, and re-try!

CONQUERING THE MOUNTAIN CALLED ME

NOTES

SHARON C. B. HUNTER

CHAPTER 11
Conquer FEAR when God's opportunity Knocks

> Then Pharaoh gave this order to all his people: "Every Hebrew boy that is born you must throw into the Nile, but let every girl live."
> Exodus 1:22

One of my favorite stories from the Bible is the birth and beginning life story of Moses. Exodus 1:22 states, "...Then Pharaoh gave this order to all his people: "Every Hebrew boy that is born you must throw into the Nile, but let every girl live." Moses was born into conflict. The verdict for his life was already death before he was even born. Yet two midwives, Shiphrah and Puah feared God and did not follow the instruction of the King of

Egypt so, they let the boys live! When Moses' mother became pregnant and gave birth, the Bible records, "...a fine son..." she hid him for three months. Before we move further with the story let's make a pit stop here. The King's verdict was clear in his instruction, "...Every Hebrew boy that is born you must throw in the Nile..." If we are going to be honest with ourselves, it can be frightening when we go against the law. However, throughout history there have been times when people stepped out and did just that. Moses' mother saw that the child was a fine child and she hid her son. She broke the law of the King. Moses' mother knew it was wrong to kill her son. However, it was also wrong to disobey the King. She had a choice to make and she chose to hide her son until the proper time. By no means am I saying go out and disobey the law. However, when we know God we understand He has a plan that stands against the plans of evil men and women. Ruthless people sometimes are in charge of the work place, organizations, and government. However, God is certain to provide a way of escape from evil decisions that bring frustration, depression, and even death. It takes courage to do what is right in the eyes of God, but wrong by the decisions of man. Yet Moses' mother, Jochebed, trusted God and he rewarded her courage and saved her son. God wants our trust in Him so we can do what's right and follow Him even if the entire world says it's wrong. My Bible tells me in 2 Thessalonians 3:3, "But the Lord is faithful, and he will strengthen you and protect you from the evil one." So, even though the King of Egypt was evil and against Jochebed, God was in her corner! Fear will push us to believe that God is not in our corner, and if we accept this thought process and listen to fear, then we will miss opportunity when it knocks. Moses' sister, Miriam, and his mother Jochebed answered the door of opportunity. When Jochebed saw that she could no longer hide her son she prepared a basket for him that would keep him safe, dry, and warm. Miriam followed the basket to see what would happen to her baby brother. The providence of God is a powerful thing. It is the means by which God directs all things. So, the courage of Jochebed to keep her son was rewarded with life! Her son lived because the daughter of the King spotted the baby among the reeds and sent her female slaves to get him. Although Pharaoh's daughter knew that the child was a Hebrew boy destined for death, the baby was crying and she took pity on him. God's Opportunity is about to knock! The Bible does not speak of Miriam's fear. It only records Miriam asking Pharaoh's daughter a question. "Shall I go and get one of the Hebrew women to nurse the baby for you." The Bible is clear in the New Testament as it states we have not because we ask not. My mother used to apply that same Scripture with this old adage, 'a closed mouth don't get fed.' We have to let go of our fear to simply ASK for what we want. Take advantage of opportunities God provides! Don't worry about what the people will say. Don't worry about the trouble you think you might get into. Just take advantage of the opportunity that God provides. The Bible does not record Pharaoh's daughter asking any questions. She saw an opportunity to have a baby and some theologians say she was barren. So, this was her chance to have a baby. She answers Miriam with two simple words, "yes, go." God's Opportunity is about to knock again! Guess who Miriam went to get to take care of her baby brother? The baby's mother, Jochebed! And to add to this already powerful story, the Bible records that once Miriam was back with the Moses' Mother who just put him out on the water, Pharaoh's daughter said to her, "Take this baby and nurse him for me, and I will pay you..." Many of the Hebrew children had died because they followed the verdict of the Pharaoh. However, Jochebed knew that this was an evil verdict and she followed God. Not only did God give her son back to enjoy the love of motherhood by taking care of and nursing her son, but she got paid to do it. The point to this story is that God seeks to give us opportunities, but if we are filled with fear we will miss the opportunity. There are so many times when we pray for God to open doors of opportunity. However, we fail to pray for the strength it will take to go through the open door. God is consistent to answer our prayers but we have to stop focusing on all of the many things that could happen once we are through the door. This thinking is futile and non-productive. However, if we pray and receive the strength to go through the door of opportunity, we will experience God's overflow of blessings. Whatever effort it takes to go against what the people say is right when God says it's wrong, always trust God! Whatever effort it takes to follow God even when it is uncomfortable, always trust God! You will find success, and He will reward your courage! Conquering fear when God's opportunity knocks will keep you living a successful life, and continuing to conquer Mountain ME!

CONQUERING THE MOUNTAIN CALLED ME

NOTES

SHARON C. B. HUNTER

CHAPTER 12
CONQUERING THE MOUNTAIN CALLED ME

2 Corinthians 5:17 "Therefore if anyone is in Christ, he is a new creature; the old things passed away; behold, new things have come."

Lamentations 3:23 "They are new every morning; great is your faithfulness."

My family always taught me the business of being beautiful is an inside job. They also taught me that this very intricate work is not something we can do alone. It takes the help of the Holy Spirit so, when we discover very unflattering idiosyncrasies about ourselves, we recognize that we need God to help us turn it around. This is what conquering the Mountain called ME is all about. Looking to

God to help us become something new in Him. As I looked back on all the things in my life that were not pleasing to God, it took me a while to decide for myself that I did not want to be consumed with all the things that glorified ugly behaviors. My heart's desire was to progress in God but God knew that the progress I wanted had its roots in knowing Jesus. Learning to understand the Word of God helped me to understand myself better. I learned that having money and things was not the epitome of success. As a matter of fact, God began to show me people who had conquered money mountains. They had all the money they needed but, they had a mountain of lack in their lives because they failed to ask God to help them overcome themselves. Therefore, they were rich in money but poor in personality, kindness, character and divine relationship. God desires for us to seek His face so that we can become the new creature in Christ. We are able to recognize the old things that have passed away because God has replaced the old with something NEW in Him. The new things that come to us by serving God, will last a lifetime.

So, as we look at the time we spent together there are things that we need to pull together so we can go forward with God and to the next place God desires to elevate us.

The issues we have are a part of living as a human being. We all have problems and issues that are not flattering as a Christian. However, we have to at least come to the mind that we have to face these issues and problems so God can fix them. Even after God shows us the things that have to be fixed with His Word, we still must make the decision to overcome our selfishness and serve God and others. Otherwise we never conquer the Mountain called ME. As we serve God we will have a greater heart and mind to follow God's ordered steps. God uses His Word like a GPS system. He shows us the direction to go in life if we keep His Word in our hearts. This heart and mind to do it God's way helps us to understand Holy living and the righteousness of God. We begin to understand that we will always make mistakes, but the sludge of the coulda's, shoulda's and woulda's do not have to keep us paralyzed and dying in the muck and mess. God wants to help us GET OVER all the IT'S of our lives. We have the opportunity to trust God and try so that we can overcome and conquer our fears. Conquering the Mountain called ME is an ongoing process. What we really conquer is the understanding that we will always need God to show us how to climb to higher personal heights. God has given us the power to become the best person that we can be and conquer the MOUNTAIN CALLED ME!

What other mountains are you ready to conquer with the help of God?

Editor's note: THIS BOOK IS A "MUST" READ FOR ANYONE WHO LOVES THE LORD AND GENUINELY WANTS TO GROW!!!!!

NOTES

www.ingramcontent.com/pod-product-compliance
Lightning Source LLC
Chambersburg PA
CBHW071212160426
43196CB00011B/2267